P9-DHI-498

SEA TURTLE JOURNEY

The Story of a Loggerhead Turtle

SMITHSONIAN OCEANIC COLLECTION

This book is for my son, Bryan, who loves the sea
and who brought joy to this journey. With love—L.A.J.

To Brian—K.L.

Original Physical Illustrations copyright © 1995 Katie Lee.
Book copyright © 1995 Trudy Corporation and the Smithsonian Institution, Washington, DC 20560.

Published by Soundprints, an imprint of Trudy Corporation, Norwalk, Connecticut.
www.soundprints.com

All rights reserved. No part of this book may be reproduced or transmitted in any form or
by any means whatsoever without prior written permission of the publisher.

Book Design: Shields & Partners, Westport, CT

First Edition 1995
10 9 8
Printed in China

A portion of the proceeds from your purchase of this licensed product supports the stated educational mission
of the Smithsonian Institution — "the increase and diffusion of knowledge."

Acknowledgments:
    Soundprints would like to thank Dr. George R. Zug of the Department of Vertebrate Zoology at the
Smithsonian's National Museum of Natural History for his curatorial review.

    Lorraine A. Jay would like to thank Paul Betournay of the Sea Turtle Preservation Society for the information
he shared and his willingness to "Talk Turtle," Dana M. Rau, editor at TMC/Soundprints, for her positive
attitude, and the members of Camp River Villa for waiting in the dark with her to watch nesting turtles.

SEA TURTLE JOURNEY
The Story of a Loggerhead Turtle

by Lorraine A. Jay   Illustrated by Katie Lee

Soundprints
Where Children Discover...

In a starry darkness, along a Florida beach, a tiny loggerhead sea turtle thrashes her way up to the surface of the sand. With dozens of brothers and dozens of sisters—bumping and pushing—the hatchling emerges from the buried nest.

A path of moonlight glimmers on the ocean. Attracted to the light, Hatchling and the others set out across the beach toward the open sea.

6

Along the dunes, a hunting raccoon prowls in the shadows of the rustling grasses. He snatches up some of the baby loggerheads as an easy meal. Ghost crabs scurrying from their burrows capture more turtles as their prey.

Hatchling and a few others escape and dive under the rolling foam. In a swimming frenzy they begin their journey to deeper waters.

7

When the first light dawns in the eastern sky, Hatchling is far from shore. Swimming near the surface, she breathes the salty air. A school of amberjack hunts the turtles in the water. Hatchling is the lucky one they do not find.

All day and through the night she swims on and on. Twenty-five miles out to sea, she climbs into a raft of seaweed. With her foreflippers tucked at her side, she sleeps in her sargassum cradle.

"*Scree! Scree!*" Hatchling awakes to the calls of swooping gulls. All around her, they pluck their dinner from the water. She hides from the birds in the bushy seaweed.

She discovers that the sargassum is like a pantry of foods—little fishes, crabs and jellyfish. Chomping on a shrimp with her tiny jaw, Loggerhead Hatchling eats her first meal.

Several years of growing pass. Loggerhead has left the open ocean to forage in coastal waters. Her shell is two feet long and spotted with algae and barnacles.

Early one day, she dives through sunlit water to a banquet on the ocean floor. She chases a calico crab. It pokes and jabs her with its claws. But Loggerhead is strong. *Crunch!* She crushes it in her powerful jaws.

At sunset, she feeds on a school of moonjellies. She doesn't see the snarl of abandoned fishing line drifting in front of her.

Loggerhead's neck and foreflippers become caught in the jumbled web. She turns and wrestles, but the line tightens. In the distance she hears the humming of an engine. A boat speeds toward her in the growing darkness.

15

Loggerhead is trapped! With all her strength, she forces her mighty foreflippers down.

Snap! The line breaks. Again she strains every muscle. Up! Down! Up! Down! She smacks the water as the boat races closer. At last, the line loosens around her. She dives, just missing the propeller as the boat zooms away.

Loggerhead swims to the surface to catch her breath. A laughing gull takes a rest from flight and settles on the water nearby. Together they drift in the gentle waves.

Night falls. Small ocean creatures shimmer in the water like a thousand diamonds. Loggerhead dives below and sleeps under the bow of a sunken wreck.

19

Year after year, Loggerhead travels through hundreds of miles of ocean waters. As she grows she explores coral reefs and basks in warm lagoons. At three-hundred pounds, she swims with grace and ease.

Late one spring, as if she knows an ancient secret, she begins her journey back to the beach where she was born. Mysteriously, she knows how to find her way.

By summer, she nears the beach and meets a male loggerhead in the waters offshore. He nuzzles her neck and they mate.

Loggerhead chooses a moonlit night and waits for high tide. Tonight, for the first time since she was a tiny hatchling, Loggerhead leaves her watery world and touches land.

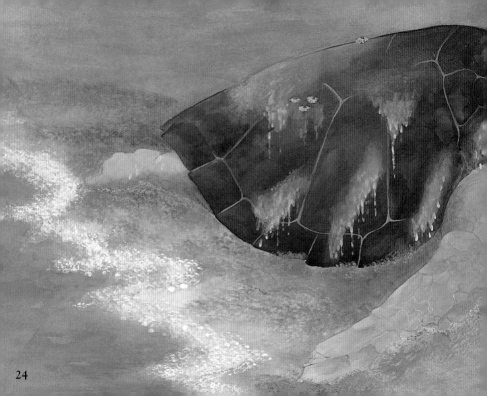

She has returned to lay her eggs in this
familiar sand. But she is alert. If an intruder
startles her, she will turn back and wait to try again.
Awkwardly, she plows across the sand to the
dune above the high tide line and stops.

Sand flies through the air.
Loggerhead's sweeping foreflippers
make a shallow crater for her huge body.
Then, she curls her hindflippers like scoopers.
Using one then the other, she digs a bottle-shaped
hole behind her.
    One hundred seven glistening white eggs
drop into the nest.

26

Like a mother tucking her babies into bed, she pats sand over her precious clutch of eggs. She takes her time. A sea turtle nest is a feast for predators, so she makes sure her eggs are well hidden. She will return to dig more nests on the beach this summer, but she will never see her hatchlings.

Now, following a moonlit path, she tracks back to the sea and disappears into the welcoming surf.

30

Two months later, under a starry sky,
a loggerhead hatchling emerges from the sand.
With all her brothers and all her sisters, she scuttles across
the beach and begins her journey to the open sea.

About the Loggerhead Sea Turtle

The loggerhead sea turtle, named for its oversized head and powerful jaw muscles, is found in temperate and subtropical waters. With a streamlined body protected by a bony shell, the loggerhead swims gracefully through the water. Unlike land turtles, the sea turtle cannot withdraw its head into its shell.

Loggerheads are solitary creatures. Leaving the beach as hatchlings, the turtles spend all their lives in the ocean. After twenty or more years, however, the female returns to her original birthplace to lay her clutch, or group, of eggs. Then every two to five years, the adult female returns to nest, laying several clutches per season. The temperature of the egg will determine whether the hatchling is male or female.

The modern species of sea turtles as we know them are an incredible four million years old, yet so much about their lives remains a mystery. Because of serious threats, including drowning in fishing nets, loss of the sea turtle's nesting habitat and the killing of sea turtles for commercial profit, it is estimated that less than one hatchling out of a thousand survives to adulthood! Many scientists, governments and private groups are working to protect these ancient reptiles and to educate people to ensure sea turtle survival.

For information about protecting sea turtles or sea turtle adoptions, please contact the Sea Turtle Survival League, c/o Caribbean Conservation Corporation, P.O. Box 2866, Gainesville, FL, 32602, or call 1-800-678-7853.

Glossary

algae: Simple green plants that live in fresh or salt water.

amberjack: A predatory fish found in warm water, swimming alone or in groups.

barnacles: Small crustaceans that attach themselves to rocks, ships and even the shells of sea turtles.

clutch: The group of eggs laid in a nest at the same time.

coral reefs: Structures built up from the ocean floor made of coraline algae and the skeletons of coral.

hatchling: A young animal recently emerged from an egg.

lagoons: Areas of shallow water separated from the sea by sandbars or reefs.

sargassum: A brown seaweed with small air bladders to help it float.